The Diplomatic Consequences of Secessionist Movements

The Diplomatic Consequences of Secessionist Movements

By Roberto Miguel Rodriguez

Economic implications: Analyzing the impact on trade, economy, and financial systems if all secessionist movements were successful in achieving independence.

The role of trade in secessionist movements

Trade plays a crucial role in secessionist movements, influencing various aspects of the economy, diplomacy, and regional power dynamics. Understanding this role is essential for diplomats and economists who seek to analyze the broader implications of successful secessionist movements.

Economic implications: Analyzing the impact on trade, economy, and financial systems if all secessionist movements were successful in achieving independence.

Successful secessionist movements can have significant economic implications, as newly independent states may face challenges in establishing trade relationships and accessing global markets. Diplomats and economists must assess the potential disruptions in supply chains, tariffs, and trade barriers that could arise from the fragmentation of a larger economic entity.

Political fragmentation: Exploring the potential consequences of multiple independent states emerging from secessionist movements, including diplomatic relations, alliances, and regional power dynamics.

Trade is intertwined with political fragmentation, influencing diplomatic relations and alliances. The emergence of multiple independent states from secessionist movements can reshape regional power dynamics, leading to shifts in trade agreements, economic partnerships, and regional integration initiatives.

Resource management: Analyzing how resource-rich regions seeking independence could impact global resource distribution, energy security, and environmental policies.

Secessionist movements in resource-rich regions have direct implications for global resource distribution, energy security, and environmental policies. Diplomats and economists must assess the potential disruption of resource flows, the establishment of new resource management systems, and the environmental impact of resource extraction within newly independent states.

International recognition: Assessing the processes and implications of international recognition of newly independent states, including their participation in global organizations and treaties.

Trade is closely linked to international recognition of newly independent states. Diplomats and economists must analyze the processes and implications of international recognition, including the participation of these states in global organizations and treaties. This recognition can impact trade relationships, access to financial resources, and the ability to negotiate trade agreements.

Socioeconomic disparities: Investigating the potential for widening disparities in wealth, development, and social services between newly independent states and their counterparts.

Secessionist movements can deepen socioeconomic disparities between newly independent states and their counterparts. Diplomats and economists must study the potential implications on wealth distribution, development, and access to social services. Trade can play a significant role in mitigating or exacerbating these disparities.

In conclusion, trade has a multifaceted role in secessionist movements. Diplomats and economists must carefully analyze the economic, political, and social implications of successful secessionist movements to understand the broader consequences for trade, diplomacy, and regional power dynamics.

Analyzing the economic impact of successful secessionist movements

Secessionist movements have become increasingly prevalent in recent times, with various regions across the globe aspiring to gain independence from their parent states. While the political, social, and cultural implications of such movements have been widely discussed, it is imperative to delve into the economic consequences that would arise if all secessionist movements were successful in achieving independence. This subchapter aims to provide diplomats and economists with a comprehensive analysis of the economic implications of successful secessionist movements.

One of the primary areas of focus is the impact on trade, economy, and financial systems. The emergence of multiple independent states would undoubtedly disrupt existing trade networks and create new economic dynamics. The subchapter will explore the potential challenges and opportunities that arise from such disruptions, including the reconfiguration of trade agreements, currency systems, and market access. Additionally, it will assess the implications for investment, foreign direct investment, and economic growth in both the newly independent states and their former parent states.

Another critical aspect to be explored is the potential consequences of political fragmentation on diplomatic relations, alliances, and regional power dynamics. The subchapter will examine how the emergence of multiple independent states would reshape existing diplomatic networks, potentially leading to the formation of new alliances and the realignment of regional power structures. It will also investigate the challenges and opportunities of establishing diplomatic relations between the newly independent states and the international community.

Furthermore, the subchapter will address the importance of cultural preservation within newly independent states resulting from secessionist movements. It will emphasize the need for promoting and protecting distinct cultures, languages, and identities, while also considering the potential economic implications of such endeavors.

Additionally, the subchapter will shed light on the national security challenges that arise from the fragmentation of states. It will analyze the potential for border disputes, defense alliances, and regional stability concerns, thereby highlighting the need for effective security arrangements and cooperation among the newly independent states.

The subchapter will also explore the impact of resource-rich regions seeking independence on global resource distribution, energy security, and environmental policies. It will analyze how the newfound control over resources can shape the economic and geopolitical landscape, as well as the potential challenges and opportunities of managing these resources sustainably.

Other important aspects to be covered include minority rights protection, governance and institution-building, international recognition, socioeconomic disparities, and the broader implications of successful secessionist movements worldwide. The subchapter aims to provide a comprehensive understanding of the economic implications of secessionist movements, enabling diplomats and economists to navigate the complex economic landscape that arises from political fragmentation.

Financial systems and currency implications

In the wake of successful secessionist movements, one crucial aspect that diplomats and economists must analyze is the impact on financial systems and currency implications. The formation of multiple independent states can have significant consequences for trade, economy, and the stability of financial systems.

One of the primary economic implications of secessionist movements is the disruption of established trade networks and economic interdependence between regions. The separation of territories can result in the creation of new borders and barriers to trade, leading to a decline in overall trade volumes and increased transaction costs. Diplomats and economists must assess the potential consequences of reduced trade on the economies of both the newly independent states and their counterparts.

Furthermore, the establishment of new currencies or the continuation of existing ones can have profound implications for financial stability. The secession of regions may require the creation of new central banks and monetary policies, which can lead to uncertainties and volatility in the financial markets. Diplomats and economists must evaluate the feasibility and sustainability of establishing independent monetary systems and the potential impact on inflation, exchange rates, and foreign investments.

In addition to the economic implications, the currency implications of secessionist movements also extend to international recognition. The recognition of a new state often involves the acknowledgment of its currency by the international community. Diplomats and economists must explore the processes and implications of international recognition, including the participation of newly independent states in global organizations and treaties.

Moreover, the secessionist movements can result in socioeconomic disparities between the newly independent states and their counterparts. Diplomats and economists must analyze the potential widening of disparities in wealth, development, and social services. These disparities can have implications for the stability and prosperity of the regions involved, as well as the potential for social unrest and conflict.

Overall, the financial systems and currency implications of successful secessionist movements are of utmost importance for diplomats and economists. Analyzing the impact on trade, economy, and financial stability, as well as the potential disparities and challenges faced by newly independent states, is essential for understanding the broader consequences of political fragmentation. By addressing these issues, diplomats and economists can contribute to the formulation of informed policies and strategies to mitigate potential risks and maximize the opportunities presented by secessionist movements.

Trade agreements and negotiations with newly independent states

When secessionist movements succeed in achieving independence, the implications are far-reaching, extending beyond the realm of politics to various economic aspects. This subchapter delves into the trade agreements and negotiations that arise with newly independent states, analyzing their impact on the global economy and financial systems.

The emergence of multiple independent states following secessionist movements necessitates the establishment of new trade agreements. Diplomats and economists must closely examine the economic implications of these agreements, assessing how they affect trade, economies, and financial systems. With the dissolution of previous political unions, such as economic communities or unions, negotiations become crucial in determining the terms of trade and ensuring the smooth flow of goods and services.

Trade agreements with newly independent states also have wider political implications. Diplomatic relations and alliances may need to be renegotiated, as these states seek to establish their position in the international community. The regional power dynamics may undergo significant shifts, as these states strive to solidify their economic and political standing.

Moreover, the preservation and promotion of distinct cultures within newly independent states are integral to their identity and development. Trade agreements must take into account the cultural preservation of these states, ensuring that their unique traditions, languages, and heritage are protected and celebrated.

While trade agreements have the potential to bring economic benefits, they can also give rise to national security challenges. Border disputes may arise between newly independent states and their former counterparts, necessitating delicate negotiations and the establishment of defense alliances. Regional stability becomes a crucial concern, as the emergence of multiple independent states can disrupt the existing balance of power.

Resource management is another key consideration in trade negotiations with newly independent states. Regions rich in resources may seek independence, impacting global resource distribution, energy security, and environmental policies. Diplomats and economists must carefully analyze the implications of these resource-rich regions gaining independence, ensuring equitable resource allocation and sustainable environmental practices.

In conclusion, the trade agreements and negotiations with newly independent states are of paramount importance. Diplomats and economists play a crucial role in analyzing the economic implications, addressing national security challenges, promoting cultural preservation, and ensuring equitable resource management. By examining these aspects, we can gain a comprehensive understanding of the broader consequences of successful secessionist movements and work towards fostering stability, inclusivity, and sustainable development in the international community.

Economic integration challenges in a fragmented political landscape

In the face of growing secessionist movements and the potential emergence of multiple independent states, the world is confronted with a range of economic integration challenges. This subchapter aims to analyze the implications of such fragmentation on trade, economy, and financial systems, offering insights to both diplomats and economists.

One of the key concerns is the impact on trade. If all secessionist movements were successful in achieving independence, the creation of multiple independent states would disrupt established trade relationships and supply chains. This would necessitate the renegotiation of trade agreements, the establishment of new customs procedures, and the potential for increased trade barriers. Diplomats and economists need to consider the potential consequences on global trade and the overall stability of the global economy.

Furthermore, the emergence of multiple independent states would have significant implications for financial systems. The division of assets and liabilities, the establishment of new currencies, and the need for financial institutions to adapt to new political realities would all present major challenges. Diplomats and economists need to assess the potential disruptions to financial markets and develop strategies to mitigate risks.

Additionally, political fragmentation raises concerns about regional power dynamics and diplomatic relations. The creation of new states can lead to shifts in alliances and the reevaluation of regional power structures. Diplomats and economists must carefully analyze the potential consequences of multiple independent states on diplomatic relations, including the formation of new alliances and the potential for conflict.

Moreover, secessionist movements often arise from a desire to preserve distinct cultures. The emergence of new states would provide an opportunity to promote and preserve these cultures. However, it is important to address potential conflicts that may arise from the protection of minority rights within newly independent states. Diplomats and economists must ensure inclusivity and work towards reconciling cultural preservation with the broader goal of national unity.

Resource management is another critical consideration. Regions seeking independence due to their resource-rich status could have significant implications for global resource distribution, energy security, and environmental policies. Diplomats and economists need to assess the potential impact on global resource markets and develop strategies to ensure equitable distribution and sustainable resource management.

In conclusion, the economic integration challenges in a fragmented political landscape are vast and multifaceted. Diplomats and economists must grapple with issues ranging from trade disruptions and financial system adaptations to regional power dynamics and cultural preservation. By addressing these challenges effectively, the global community can navigate the complex terrain of secessionist movements and work towards a more stable and prosperous future.

Chapter 2: Political fragmentation: Exploring the potential consequences of multiple independent states emerging from secessionist movements, including diplomatic relations, alliances, and regional power dynamics.

Diplomatic relations and recognition of newly independent states

The process of secession and the subsequent emergence of newly independent states have far-reaching diplomatic consequences. This subchapter explores the intricacies of diplomatic relations and the recognition of these newly independent states. Addressing an audience of diplomats and economists, this section delves into the complexities of navigating international relations in the wake of successful secessionist movements.

The recognition of newly independent states is a critical aspect of their integration into the global community. This subchapter analyzes the processes and implications of international recognition, including the participation of these states in global organizations and treaties. It delves into the challenges and opportunities of establishing diplomatic ties with other nations, negotiating bilateral agreements, and forging alliances to ensure regional stability.

Furthermore, the subchapter explores the potential consequences of multiple independent states emerging from secessionist movements. It examines the shifting power dynamics within regions, the reconfiguration of alliances, and the impact on global politics. The economic implications of these secessionist movements are also explored, analyzing the impact on trade, economy, and financial systems if all secessionist movements were successful.

Cultural preservation is another crucial aspect addressed in this subchapter. It focuses on the preservation and promotion of distinct cultures within newly independent states resulting from secessionist movements. The exploration of cultural preservation aims to ensure the recognition and protection of cultural diversity as a valuable asset in the global arena.

The security implications of multiple independent states are also investigated, including border disputes, defense alliances, and regional stability. This section assesses the challenges of maintaining security in a fragmented geopolitical landscape and explores potential solutions to mitigate conflicts and ensure peace.

In addition, the subchapter delves into the challenges and opportunities of governance and institution-building in these newly independent states. It examines the process of establishing new governments, legal systems, and institutions in the aftermath of successful secessionist movements.

Lastly, this subchapter investigates the wider implications of successful secessionist movements worldwide. It explores the rise of nationalism, the reshaping of global governance structures, and the impact on international relations. The potential for widening socioeconomic disparities between newly independent states and their counterparts is also examined.

Overall, this subchapter provides diplomats and economists with a comprehensive analysis of the diplomatic relations and recognition of newly independent states. It addresses the economic, political, cultural, and security implications of secessionist movements, providing valuable insights for navigating the complex terrain of international relations in a fragmented world.

Alliances and regional power shifts

Alliances and regional power shifts are crucial aspects of the diplomatic consequences that arise from secessionist movements. As diplomats and economists, it is essential to understand the implications of these shifts in order to effectively navigate the ever-changing global landscape. This subchapter will explore the potential consequences of multiple independent states emerging from secessionist movements, focusing on diplomatic relations, alliances, and regional power dynamics.

The emergence of independent states resulting from secessionist movements can significantly impact diplomatic relations. With new states entering the global stage, existing diplomatic alliances and partnerships may need to be reevaluated. Traditional political blocs and alliances may undergo transformations as these newly independent states seek to redefine their diplomatic priorities and establish their own international standing.

Moreover, regional power dynamics can undergo significant shifts as secessionist movements succeed. The creation of multiple independent states can disrupt the existing balance of power within a region, leading to potential rivalries and conflicts. This can also result in the formation of new regional alliances as states seek to strengthen their positions and protect their interests.

The economic implications of these shifts are also noteworthy. Trade, economy, and financial systems can be greatly affected if all secessionist movements were successful. The establishment of new borders and trade regulations can disrupt established economic networks, leading to potential declines in trade and investment. Additionally, the division of resources among newly independent states can create economic disparities, impacting regional stability and development.

Furthermore, the preservation and promotion of distinct cultures within newly independent states must be taken into consideration. The successful secession of regions with strong cultural identities can result in the formation of new states that prioritize the preservation and promotion of their unique cultures. This poses challenges as well as opportunities for diplomats and economists in terms of fostering cultural diversity and inclusivity, while also ensuring the protection of minority rights.

In conclusion, the subchapter "Alliances and regional power shifts" delves into the diplomatic consequences of secessionist movements. It highlights the potential disruptions in diplomatic relations, formation of new alliances, and shifts in regional power dynamics. Additionally, it emphasizes the economic implications, cultural preservation, national security challenges, resource management, minority rights, governance and institution-building, international recognition, socioeconomic disparities, and the broader global trend of secessionist movements. By understanding these consequences, diplomats and economists can better navigate the complexities of a world where secessionist movements succeed.

Implications for global governance structures

As secessionist movements gain momentum worldwide, the implications for global governance structures cannot be overlooked. Diplomats and economists must carefully analyze the potential consequences of these movements, considering various aspects such as economic implications, political fragmentation, cultural preservation, national security challenges, resource management, minority rights, governance and institution-building, international recognition, socioeconomic disparities, and the broader trend of secessionist movements as a global phenomenon.

Economic implications are of paramount importance when assessing the impact of successful secessionist movements. Analyzing the potential effects on trade, economy, and financial systems is crucial. If all secessionist movements were to achieve independence, it would disrupt established economic relationships and necessitate the creation of new trade agreements and economic partnerships. Diplomats and economists must explore the potential consequences to ensure economic stability and growth.

Political fragmentation resulting from secessionist movements raises concerns regarding diplomatic relations, alliances, and regional power dynamics. The emergence of multiple independent states could lead to the reconfiguration of global political alliances and power structures. Understanding these potential consequences is vital for diplomats and economists to navigate the changing geopolitical landscape.

Cultural preservation is another critical aspect to address. Newly independent states resulting from secessionist movements often strive to preserve and promote their distinct cultures. Diplomats and economists should support efforts to safeguard cultural heritage and foster inclusivity within these states.

National security challenges arise with the emergence of multiple independent states. Border disputes, defense alliances, and regional stability could all be affected. A comprehensive analysis of the security implications is necessary to ensure peace and stability in the region.

Resource management is another crucial consideration. Resource-rich regions seeking independence could impact global resource distribution, energy security, and environmental policies. Diplomats and economists must assess the potential consequences and devise strategies to ensure sustainable resource management.

Protecting minority rights within newly independent states is essential to prevent conflicts and ensure inclusivity. Diplomats and economists should explore mechanisms to safeguard minority rights and promote social cohesion in these states.

The challenges and opportunities of establishing new governments, legal systems, and institutions after successful secessionist movements must be carefully examined. Diplomats and economists should provide guidance and support to facilitate effective governance and institution-building processes.

International recognition of newly independent states and their participation in global organizations and treaties is another significant consideration. Assessing the processes and implications of international recognition is crucial for diplomats and economists to navigate the evolving global landscape.

Socioeconomic disparities between newly independent states and their counterparts could widen as a result of secessionist movements. Diplomats and economists should identify strategies to address these disparities and ensure equitable development and access to social services.

Lastly, the broader implications of secessionist movements as a global trend must be examined. The impact on international relations, the rise of nationalism, and the reshaping of global governance structures should be carefully analyzed.

In conclusion, the implications for global governance structures resulting from secessionist movements are multifaceted and require thorough analysis. Diplomats and economists must address economic, political, cultural, security, and resource-related aspects, along with minority rights, governance, international recognition, socioeconomic disparities, and the broader trend of secessionist movements. By understanding these implications, diplomats and economists can navigate the changing global landscape and promote stability, inclusivity, and sustainable development.

Negotiating diplomatic challenges in a fragmented political landscape

In a world where secessionist movements are gaining momentum, diplomats and economists face unprecedented challenges in navigating the complexities of a fragmented political landscape. This subchapter delves into the key diplomatic challenges that arise when multiple independent states emerge from secessionist movements, exploring various aspects such as economic implications, political fragmentation, cultural preservation, national security challenges, resource management, minority rights, governance and institution-building, international recognition, socioeconomic disparities, and the broader global trend of secessionist movements.

One of the most crucial issues that diplomats and economists must address is the economic implications of secessionist movements. Analyzing the impact on trade, economy, and financial systems if all secessionist movements were successful in achieving independence is of utmost importance. This entails evaluating the potential disruptions to global supply chains, market access, and investment flows, as well as the implications for regional economic integration and cooperation.

Moreover, the subchapter explores the potential consequences of political fragmentation resulting from secessionist movements. This includes examining the diplomatic relations, alliances, and regional power dynamics that may emerge as multiple independent states assert their sovereignty. It further analyzes the challenges and opportunities of establishing new governments, legal systems, and institutions in the wake of successful secessionist movements.

Cultural preservation is another critical aspect that diplomats and economists need to address. The subchapter delves into the preservation and promotion of distinct cultures within newly independent states, highlighting the importance of fostering inclusivity and ensuring the protection of minority rights. It also investigates potential conflicts that may arise between different cultural groups and explores strategies for maintaining social cohesion.

The subchapter also delves into the national security challenges posed by multiple independent states. This includes examining potential border disputes, defense alliances, and the overall regional stability implications of secessionist movements. It further explores the impact on global resource distribution, energy security, and environmental policies that may arise if resource-rich regions seeking independence successfully achieve their goals.

Furthermore, the subchapter assesses the processes and implications of international recognition of newly independent states. This includes analyzing their participation in global organizations and treaties, as well as the broader implications for international relations and the reshaping of global governance structures. It also investigates the potential widening disparities in wealth, development, and social services between newly independent states and their counterparts, and explores strategies for addressing these socioeconomic disparities.

In conclusion, negotiating diplomatic challenges in a fragmented political landscape is a multifaceted task that requires careful analysis and strategic decision-making. This subchapter provides a comprehensive exploration of the various challenges and opportunities that diplomats and economists must confront in the face of secessionist movements, offering valuable insights for navigating this complex terrain.

Chapter 3: Cultural preservation: Focusing on the preservation and promotion of distinct cultures within newly independent states resulting from secessionist movements.

Cultural diversity and identity within secessionist movements

In the modern world, secessionist movements have become a global phenomenon, challenging the existing political order and reshaping the dynamics of international relations. As diplomats and economists, it is crucial to understand the various implications that arise from these movements, particularly when it comes to cultural diversity and identity within newly independent states.

One of the key aspects to consider is the preservation and promotion of distinct cultures within these states. Secessionist movements often arise due to cultural differences and the desire for self-determination. Therefore, it is essential to examine how these newly independent states can ensure the protection of minority cultures and their inclusion in the decision-making processes. Addressing potential conflicts and establishing inclusive policies will be critical to maintaining social cohesion and stability.

Another important consideration is the impact on national security challenges. With the emergence of multiple independent states, border disputes, defense alliances, and regional stability become major concerns. Diplomats and economists must analyze these factors and work towards establishing mechanisms that ensure peaceful relations between these newly independent states, so as to avoid potential conflicts and maintain regional stability.

Moreover, the governance and institution-building in the wake of successful secessionist movements pose both challenges and opportunities. Establishing new governments, legal systems, and institutions can be complex tasks, especially in regions with diverse cultural backgrounds. Diplomats and economists need to provide guidance and support to these states in order to foster effective governance that caters to the needs and aspirations of all citizens.

Furthermore, the international recognition of newly independent states is a crucial aspect to consider. Assessing the processes and implications of such recognition, including their participation in global organizations and treaties, is essential for the smooth integration of these states into the international community. Diplomats and economists must navigate the complexities of international relations to ensure that these states are given the opportunity to participate and contribute to global governance structures.

Lastly, secessionist movements have the potential to widen socioeconomic disparities between newly independent states and their counterparts. Examining the potential for disparities in wealth, development, and social services is crucial in order to address these challenges and promote equitable growth and development.

In conclusion, understanding the cultural diversity and identity within secessionist movements is essential for diplomats and economists. By focusing on areas such as cultural preservation, national security challenges, governance and institution-building, international recognition, and socioeconomic disparities, we can better analyze the consequences of these movements and develop strategies to address the challenges and opportunities that arise from them. This will ultimately contribute to maintaining diplomatic relations, regional stability, and inclusive development in the wake of successful secessionist movements.

Challenges in preserving cultural heritage

Preserving cultural heritage is a significant challenge that arises when secessionist movements successfully achieve independence, leading to the emergence of multiple independent states. This subchapter aims to address the concerns surrounding cultural preservation within these newly independent states and the potential consequences for diplomatic relations, regional power dynamics, and alliances.

Cultural preservation plays a crucial role in maintaining the distinct identities and traditions of communities within these newly independent states. However, the process becomes complex as secessionist movements often arise from deep-rooted ethnic, linguistic, or religious differences. These differences can create tensions and conflicts, making it challenging to strike a balance between the preservation of cultural heritage and the need for national unity.

One of the primary challenges in cultural preservation is the protection of minority rights. Secessionist movements often result in the formation of states where minority communities find themselves in the minority once again. Ensuring inclusivity and safeguarding the rights of these minority groups becomes paramount to prevent discrimination and social unrest.

Another challenge lies in governance and institution-building. Establishing new governments, legal systems, and institutions in the wake of successful secessionist movements requires careful planning and execution. The preservation of cultural heritage should be integrated into the fabric of these new institutions to promote diversity and inclusivity.

International recognition adds another layer of complexity. The processes and implications of international recognition of newly independent states have a direct impact on their participation in global organizations and treaties. The recognition of these states as independent entities can provide opportunities for cultural preservation through participation in global cultural exchange programs. However, it can also create diplomatic tensions if the international community questions the legitimacy of these states.

Furthermore, cultural preservation within newly independent states can have economic implications. Distinct cultures attract tourism, which can be an important source of revenue for these states. However, challenges such as infrastructural development, marketing, and sustainable tourism practices need to be carefully addressed to maximize the economic benefits without compromising cultural integrity.

In conclusion, preserving cultural heritage within newly independent states resulting from secessionist movements poses several challenges. These challenges encompass minority rights protection, governance and institution-building, international recognition, and economic implications. Overcoming these challenges requires a balanced approach that acknowledges the importance of cultural heritage while fostering inclusivity, promoting economic growth, and maintaining diplomatic relations with the international community. Diplomats and economists play a crucial role in navigating these challenges to ensure the preservation and promotion of distinct cultures within the context of political fragmentation.

Cultural policies and initiatives in newly independent states

In the wake of successful secessionist movements, newly independent states face a myriad of challenges and opportunities. One crucial aspect that demands attention is the preservation and promotion of distinct cultures within these states. Cultural preservation not only safeguards the rich heritage and traditions of these regions but also contributes to their overall development and identity. This subchapter delves into the cultural policies and initiatives that can be implemented in newly independent states to ensure the preservation and promotion of their unique cultures.

Cultural preservation plays a pivotal role in fostering a sense of pride and unity among the citizens of newly independent states. By recognizing and celebrating their diverse cultural identities, these states can create a harmonious society that values inclusivity and pluralism. Diplomats and economists must understand the significance of cultural initiatives in promoting social cohesion and stability within these states.

One approach to cultural preservation is the establishment of cultural institutions and organizations that cater to the specific needs of each region. These institutions can play a crucial role in organizing cultural events, festivals, and exhibitions that showcase the artistic and intellectual achievements of the region. Moreover, they can support local artists, musicians, and writers by providing them with platforms to showcase their talents and nurture their creativity.

Another essential aspect of cultural preservation is the protection of minority rights within newly independent states. Inclusivity must be at the forefront of governance and institution-building processes. Efforts should be made to ensure that minority communities are not marginalized or excluded from the cultural fabric of these states. This includes promoting cultural diversity in educational curricula, providing language rights, and facilitating the participation of minority groups in decision-making processes.

International recognition also plays a crucial role in supporting cultural preservation in newly independent states. By participating in global organizations and treaties, these states can enhance their cultural diplomacy efforts, foster international collaborations, and gain access to resources that can aid in the preservation and promotion of their distinct cultures.

Furthermore, economic implications cannot be overlooked in the pursuit of cultural preservation. Diplomats and economists must analyze the impact of cultural policies and initiatives on trade, economy, and financial systems. They should explore how cultural tourism, creative industries, and cultural exchange programs can contribute to economic growth and development in these states.

In conclusion, cultural preservation is a vital aspect of nation-building in newly independent states resulting from secessionist movements. By formulating comprehensive cultural policies and implementing initiatives that protect and promote distinct cultures, these states can foster social cohesion, enhance international recognition, and contribute to their overall development and identity. Diplomats and economists play a crucial role in analyzing the economic implications, understanding the political fragmentation, and exploring the potential consequences of multiple independent states emerging from secessionist movements, ultimately shaping the future of these newly independent states.

Promoting cultural exchange and understanding in a fragmented political landscape

In the wake of successful secessionist movements, one of the most pressing challenges is to promote cultural exchange and understanding within the newly independent states. The fragmentation of political landscapes often leads to the formation of multiple states with distinct cultures and identities. It is crucial for diplomats and economists to address this issue in order to foster peaceful coexistence, promote inclusivity, and prevent potential conflicts.

Cultural preservation plays a vital role in maintaining the identity of these newly independent states. By focusing on the preservation and promotion of distinct cultures, diplomats and economists can help bridge the gaps between these states and encourage mutual respect and understanding. Strategies such as cultural exchange programs, educational initiatives, and cultural festivals can facilitate interaction and dialogue among diverse communities.

However, cultural exchange should not be limited to the newly independent states alone. Efforts should also be made to encourage cross-border cultural interactions and collaborations. By organizing cultural events, exhibitions, and artistic exchanges, diplomats and economists can create platforms for people from different states to come together, celebrate their shared heritage, and appreciate their differences.

Moreover, it is important to address the protection of minority rights within these newly independent states. Secessionist movements often lead to questions regarding the status and rights of minority communities. Diplomats and economists must work towards ensuring inclusivity and preventing any marginalization or discrimination. Policies that safeguard minority rights, promote cultural diversity, and encourage participation in decision-making processes should be prioritized.

To effectively promote cultural exchange and understanding, it is essential to establish institutions and frameworks that facilitate dialogue and cooperation. Diplomats and economists can support the establishment of cultural exchange centers, research institutes, and platforms for intercultural dialogue. These initiatives can encourage collaboration, foster understanding, and contribute to the development of peaceful relations among the newly independent states.

In conclusion, promoting cultural exchange and understanding is crucial in a fragmented political landscape. Diplomats and economists must prioritize cultural preservation, protection of minority rights, and the establishment of institutions to facilitate dialogue and cooperation. By fostering mutual respect and understanding, they can contribute to the peaceful coexistence and development of these newly independent states.

Chapter 4: National security challenges: Examining the security implications of multiple independent states emerging, including border disputes, defense alliances, and regional stability.

Border disputes and territorial claims

Border disputes and territorial claims are a significant aspect of analyzing the impact of secessionist movements on global diplomacy and economics. As diplomats and economists navigate the complex landscape of political fragmentation, understanding the implications of these disputes is crucial. This subchapter delves into the various dimensions of border disputes and territorial claims that arise from successful secessionist movements.

One of the economic implications of border disputes is the potential disruption of trade and financial systems. As newly independent states emerge, questions about the movement of goods and services across borders become paramount. Existing trade agreements and economic partnerships may need to be renegotiated, leading to uncertainty and potential economic downturns. Economists must assess the impact on trade, economy, and financial systems if all secessionist movements were successful in achieving independence.

Furthermore, border disputes have profound political consequences. Diplomatic relations, alliances, and regional power dynamics undergo significant shifts when multiple independent states emerge. Diplomats must navigate the complexities of establishing new relationships and negotiating treaties to ensure stability and cooperation in the region.

Cultural preservation is another critical aspect related to border disputes and territorial claims. As new states emerge, the promotion and preservation of distinct cultures within these territories become essential. Diplomats and economists must consider how these cultural differences impact social cohesion, national identity, and inclusivity within these newly independent states.

Border disputes also pose national security challenges. The emergence of multiple independent states can lead to conflicts over territorial boundaries, defense alliances, and regional stability. Diplomats and economists need to address these security implications to prevent potential conflicts and maintain regional peace.

Resource management is another crucial consideration. Regions rich in resources seeking independence can impact global resource distribution, energy security, and environmental policies. Diplomats and economists must analyze the implications of these resource-rich regions becoming independent and develop strategies to ensure fair and sustainable resource management.

Additionally, the protection of minority rights within newly independent states is of utmost importance. Diplomats and economists must investigate potential conflicts and ensure inclusivity to prevent discrimination and social unrest.

Governance and institution-building are significant challenges that arise from successful secessionist movements. Establishing new governments, legal systems, and institutions requires careful planning and coordination. Diplomats and economists must explore the challenges and opportunities in building these institutions to ensure stability and effective governance.

International recognition is a crucial aspect that diplomats and economists must assess. The processes and implications of international recognition of newly independent states, including their participation in global organizations and treaties, have far-reaching consequences for their diplomatic and economic standing.

Furthermore, socio-economic disparities between newly independent states and their counterparts must be investigated. These disparities can lead to widening gaps in wealth, development, and social services. Diplomats and economists need to identify strategies to address these disparities and promote equitable development.

Finally, this subchapter examines secessionist movements as a global trend and its broader implications. The rise of nationalism, the reshaping of global governance structures, and the impact on international relations are all vital considerations for diplomats and economists.

In conclusion, border disputes and territorial claims resulting from secessionist movements have significant implications for diplomats and economists. Understanding these implications is crucial for addressing economic, political, cultural, security, governance, resource management, minority rights, international recognition, socio-economic disparities, and global trends. By delving into these dimensions, diplomats and economists can navigate the complexities and challenges of political fragmentation successfully.

Defense alliances and security cooperation

Defense alliances and security cooperation are critical aspects to consider when analyzing the consequences of secessionist movements. As secessionist movements gain momentum and result in the formation of multiple independent states, the security landscape undergoes significant changes, affecting regional stability, border disputes, and international relations. This subchapter delves into the national security challenges posed by the emergence of independent states, highlighting the need for defense alliances and security cooperation in this new geopolitical context.

The successful achievement of independence by secessionist movements has profound implications for national security. The borders of newly independent states may become subject to disputes, as neighboring countries assert claims over territories or resources. This can potentially escalate into conflicts, threatening regional stability and necessitating the establishment of defense alliances.

Defense alliances play a crucial role in maintaining security and deterring potential aggressors. As multiple independent states emerge, the need for mutual defense becomes paramount. Diplomats and economists must understand the importance of fostering alliances and cooperation agreements to ensure the security of these newly independent states.

Regional power dynamics also undergo significant shifts when secessionist movements succeed. The emergence of new states may disrupt existing power structures and alliances, leading to realignments and diplomatic recalibrations. Understanding these dynamics is essential for diplomats and economists to navigate the changing geopolitical landscape effectively.

Furthermore, this subchapter explores the potential for defense alliances and security cooperation to promote stability and peacebuilding. By forging alliances and cooperating on security matters, newly independent states can mitigate the risks of conflict and work towards regional stability. This entails establishing mechanisms for intelligence sharing, joint military exercises, and coordinated responses to security threats.

Overall, defense alliances and security cooperation are critical components to consider when analyzing the consequences of secessionist movements. Diplomats and economists need to understand the security implications of multiple independent states emerging and work towards fostering alliances and cooperation agreements to ensure regional stability and promote peacebuilding efforts. By doing so, they can contribute to a more secure and prosperous future for these newly independent states, while also addressing the broader challenges and opportunities that arise from secessionist movements worldwide.

Maintaining regional stability in a fragmented political landscape

In the rapidly changing global landscape, secessionist movements are becoming increasingly prevalent, leading to a fragmented political landscape. As diplomats and economists, it is crucial to understand the potential consequences of such movements and work towards maintaining regional stability. This subchapter aims to explore the various aspects related to this issue, including economic implications, political fragmentation, cultural preservation, national security challenges, resource management, minority rights, governance and institution-building, international recognition, socioeconomic disparities, and secessionist movements as a global trend.

Economic implications play a significant role in analyzing the impact of successful secessionist movements on trade, economy, and financial systems. The emergence of multiple independent states can disrupt established trade routes, introduce new regulatory frameworks, and potentially lead to economic instability. It is essential to examine the potential consequences and develop strategies to mitigate any negative effects.

Political fragmentation resulting from secessionist movements has far-reaching implications for diplomatic relations, alliances, and regional power dynamics. The emergence of new states can reshape existing geopolitical structures and lead to shifting alliances, which require careful analysis and strategic decision-making.

Cultural preservation is another critical aspect that needs to be addressed when discussing secessionist movements. The promotion and preservation of distinct cultures within newly independent states are essential for ensuring inclusivity and harmonious coexistence.

National security challenges arise from the emergence of multiple independent states, including border disputes, defense alliances, and regional stability. It is crucial to assess the potential security implications and develop mechanisms to address them effectively.

Resource management is another crucial area of concern. Resource-rich regions seeking independence can impact global resource distribution, energy security, and environmental policies. Analyzing and addressing these issues is vital for sustainable development and global stability.

The protection of minority rights within newly independent states is crucial for ensuring a harmonious transition. Investigating potential conflicts and devising inclusive policies are essential for maintaining social cohesion and stability.

Establishing new governments, legal systems, and institutions is a significant challenge in the wake of successful secessionist movements. Analyzing the challenges and opportunities of governance and institution-building is vital for ensuring effective administration and stability.

Assessing the processes and implications of international recognition of newly independent states is crucial. Understanding their participation in global organizations and treaties is essential for promoting cooperation and global stability.

Socioeconomic disparities between newly independent states and their counterparts can widen after secession. Investigating these potential disparities and implementing policies to address them is essential for promoting inclusive development and stability.

Finally, examining secessionist movements as a global trend is essential for understanding their broader implications. This includes the impact on international relations, the rise of nationalism, and the reshaping of global governance structures.

In conclusion, maintaining regional stability in a fragmented political landscape requires a comprehensive understanding of the various consequences of secessionist movements. This subchapter delves into the economic, political, cultural, security, resource management, minority rights, governance, international recognition, socioeconomic disparities, and global implications of successful secessionist movements. By addressing these issues, diplomats and economists can contribute to promoting stability and harmony in a rapidly changing world.

Resolving conflicts and promoting peaceful coexistence

In the complex landscape of political fragmentation caused by secessionist movements, resolving conflicts and promoting peaceful coexistence becomes a crucial task for diplomats and economists. This subchapter delves into the various aspects of conflict resolution and the promotion of harmonious relationships between new independent states and their counterparts.

Conflicts arising from secessionist movements often stem from deep-rooted grievances, ethnic tensions, and territorial disputes. Diplomats and economists must actively engage in dialogue and negotiation to address these issues and find mutually acceptable solutions. Mediation and arbitration can play a significant role in resolving border disputes and ensuring territorial integrity. Additionally, establishing regional mechanisms and organizations for conflict prevention and resolution can help maintain stability and foster cooperation.

Promoting peaceful coexistence also requires addressing the concerns of minority groups within newly independent states. Protection of minority rights, inclusivity, and equal representation are essential elements in fostering a harmonious society. Diplomats and economists must work closely with local governments and civil society organizations to ensure the inclusion and empowerment of minority communities. Furthermore, promoting cultural diversity and preserving distinct cultures within these states can contribute to social cohesion and mutual respect.

Moreover, economic interdependence and trade relations play a vital role in maintaining peaceful coexistence. By analyzing the impact on trade, economy, and financial systems if all secessionist movements were successful, diplomats and economists can identify potential areas of conflict and develop strategies to minimize disruptions. Establishing regional economic agreements and trade blocs can promote economic cooperation and mitigate potential trade disputes.

Institution-building and governance are also critical in ensuring stability and peaceful coexistence. Diplomats and economists can provide expertise in establishing new governments, legal systems, and institutions that are inclusive, transparent, and accountable. Capacity-building programs can be implemented to support the effective functioning of these institutions, fostering good governance and the rule of law.

Lastly, international recognition of newly independent states plays a significant role in promoting peaceful coexistence. Diplomats and economists can assess the processes and implications of international recognition, including the participation of these states in global organizations and treaties. Encouraging dialogue and cooperation among these states and their counterparts on regional and global platforms can foster understanding and build trust.

In conclusion, resolving conflicts and promoting peaceful coexistence is a multifaceted endeavor that requires the active involvement of diplomats and economists. By addressing issues such as minority rights, economic interdependence, institution-building, and international recognition, they can contribute to the stability and harmony of newly independent states resulting from secessionist movements.

Chapter 5: Resource management: Analyzing how resource-rich regions seeking independence could impact global resource distribution, energy security, and environmental policies.

Resource-rich regions and secessionist movements

Resource-rich regions seeking independence pose unique challenges and opportunities for diplomats and economists. This subchapter delves into the economic, political, cultural, and environmental implications of secessionist movements in such regions, shedding light on the broader consequences for global governance and international relations.

One of the primary concerns when analyzing the impact of successful secessionist movements is the economic implications. This section explores the potential effects on trade, economy, and financial systems if all secessionist movements were to achieve independence. It delves into the challenges and opportunities that arise from the emergence of multiple independent states, including the reconfiguration of trade relationships, the establishment of new economic frameworks, and the redistribution of resources.

Political fragmentation resulting from secessionist movements is another critical aspect to consider. This subchapter explores the potential consequences of multiple independent states emerging, including the reconfiguration of diplomatic relations, the formation of new alliances, and the dynamics of regional power. It highlights the challenges of maintaining stability in a world where the geopolitical landscape is continually evolving.

Cultural preservation is of paramount importance within newly independent states resulting from secessionist movements. This section emphasizes the need to protect and promote distinct cultures, languages, and traditions, ensuring their viability and inclusivity in the global arena. It examines the challenges of balancing cultural preservation with the necessity of adapting to a rapidly changing world.

National security challenges are inherent in the emergence of multiple independent states. This subchapter investigates the security implications, including potential border disputes, the formation of defense alliances, and the overall regional stability. It underscores the importance of managing these challenges effectively to avoid conflicts that could disrupt global security.

The impact on resource distribution, energy security, and environmental policies is another critical aspect to explore. This section analyzes how resource-rich regions seeking independence can influence global resource management and energy security. It also emphasizes the need for sustainable environmental policies in newly independent states.

Minority rights are crucial within newly independent states, and this section investigates the protection of minority rights, addressing potential conflicts and ensuring inclusivity. It explores the challenges of maintaining harmony and social cohesion while celebrating diversity.

Governance and institution-building are also examined in this subchapter. It explores the challenges and opportunities of establishing new governments, legal systems, and institutions in the wake of successful secessionist movements. It emphasizes the importance of building robust and inclusive institutions to ensure the long-term stability and prosperity of newly independent states.

The processes and implications of international recognition of newly independent states are assessed in terms of their participation in global organizations and treaties. This section delves into the diplomatic aspects of international recognition and the potential consequences for global governance structures.

Socioeconomic disparities between newly independent states and their counterparts are investigated, focusing on the potential for widening disparities in wealth, development, and social services. It highlights the importance of addressing these disparities to ensure equitable growth and development.

Finally, this subchapter broadens the scope to examine secessionist movements as a global trend. It explores the broader implications of successful secessionist movements worldwide, including their impact on international relations, the rise of nationalism, and the reshaping of global governance structures.

In summary, this subchapter delves into the multifaceted consequences of resource-rich regions seeking independence through secessionist movements. By addressing economic, political, cultural, environmental, and social aspects, it provides diplomats and economists with a comprehensive understanding of the challenges and opportunities associated with such movements and their impact on global dynamics.

Global resource distribution and its impact on newly independent states

Global resource distribution plays a crucial role in shaping the economic and geopolitical landscape of the world. The impact of this distribution on newly independent states resulting from secessionist movements cannot be understated. In this subchapter, we will delve into the intricate relationship between resource management and its implications for these states, as well as for global resource distribution, energy security, and environmental policies.

The process of secession often involves regions that possess abundant natural resources seeking independence. These regions could potentially disrupt the established global resource distribution patterns, which have been shaped by decades of geopolitical alliances and interests. As diplomats and economists, it is essential to analyze and understand the potential consequences of such disruptions.

The successful independence of resource-rich regions could have far-reaching economic implications. The impact on trade, economy, and financial systems would be significant. It is crucial to assess how these newly independent states would adapt to the global market, and how their newfound autonomy might affect their economic development. Additionally, the redistribution of resources could lead to shifts in regional power dynamics and alter the balance of economic influence.

Energy security is another critical aspect to consider. Resource-rich regions seeking independence might have control over vital energy resources, such as oil, gas, or minerals. The geopolitical implications of this control could have ripple effects on global energy markets and energy security. It is paramount to analyze the potential consequences and develop strategies to ensure the stability and availability of energy resources.

Furthermore, the environmental policies of newly independent states must be considered. These regions may have different approaches to environmental conservation and sustainability, which could impact global environmental policies. Examining the environmental implications of resource-rich regions seeking independence is crucial for understanding the potential challenges and opportunities in addressing climate change and promoting sustainable development.

In conclusion, the impact of global resource distribution on newly independent states resulting from secessionist movements is a complex and multifaceted issue. As diplomats and economists, it is our responsibility to analyze the potential consequences for trade, economy, and financial systems, energy security, environmental policies, and regional power dynamics. By understanding and addressing these challenges, we can contribute to the sustainable development and stability of both the newly independent states and the global community as a whole.

Energy security implications in a fragmented political landscape

In a world marked by political fragmentation resulting from secessionist movements, energy security becomes a critical concern for diplomats and economists. The emergence of multiple independent states can have significant implications for global resource distribution, environmental policies, regional stability, and economic development.

One of the primary concerns in a fragmented political landscape is the impact on energy distribution and access. Resource-rich regions seeking independence may disrupt global resource distribution, potentially leading to heightened competition and conflicts over energy sources. This, in turn, can affect energy prices and availability, affecting global economies and trade relations.

Moreover, the establishment of new governments and legal systems in newly independent states poses challenges in energy governance and institution-building. Ensuring transparent and effective energy policies, regulations, and institutions become crucial to maintaining stability and attracting investments in the energy sector.

Border disputes and defense alliances also become significant factors influencing energy security in a fragmented political landscape. As multiple independent states emerge, border demarcations and control over energy infrastructure can become contentious issues, potentially leading to geopolitical tensions and conflicts. The formation of defense alliances to safeguard energy resources and infrastructure may further complicate diplomatic relations and regional power dynamics.

Furthermore, the environmental implications of energy production and consumption cannot be overlooked. As regions seeking independence may be resource-rich, their exploitation can have significant environmental consequences, including increased carbon emissions, habitat destruction, and water scarcity. Balancing the energy needs of newly independent states with sustainable environmental policies becomes imperative.

Finally, the impact on global energy markets and investments cannot be ignored. The successful secessionist movements worldwide can reshape the global energy landscape, affecting investment patterns and market dynamics. Diplomats and economists must closely analyze the potential economic implications, including trade, financial systems, and investment flows, if all secessionist movements were to achieve independence.

In conclusion, energy security implications in a fragmented political landscape are multifaceted and require careful analysis by diplomats and economists. The consequences of multiple independent states emerging from secessionist movements extend beyond energy distribution and access to encompass geopolitical tensions, environmental sustainability, economic development, and global investment patterns. Addressing these challenges will require proactive diplomacy, cooperation, and the formulation of innovative energy policies to ensure a stable and sustainable energy future.

Environmental policies and sustainable development challenges

As secessionist movements gain momentum worldwide, it is crucial to examine the potential environmental and sustainable development challenges that may arise from the emergence of multiple independent states. This subchapter delves into the implications of resource-rich regions seeking independence, analyzing how it could impact global resource distribution, energy security, and environmental policies.

The successful attainment of independence by resource-rich regions could have far-reaching consequences for trade, economy, and financial systems. These regions often possess significant reserves of natural resources, such as oil, gas, minerals, or fertile land. Their secession could disrupt existing trade routes and supply chains, leading to economic instability and market fluctuations. Moreover, the newfound control over resources may incentivize these newly independent states to prioritize their own economic growth, potentially disregarding environmental concerns and sustainable development practices.

Energy security is another crucial aspect to consider. Resource-rich regions seeking independence may become key players in the global energy market, potentially altering the dynamics of energy distribution and supply. This could have implications for energy-dependent countries, as they may have to adapt their energy policies and diversify their sources to secure a stable supply.

Furthermore, the emergence of multiple independent states can lead to fragmented environmental policies. Each state may adopt its own set of regulations and priorities, potentially resulting in an inconsistent approach to environmental protection. This could hinder international efforts to address global challenges such as climate change, deforestation, or pollution. Diplomatic coordination and cooperation will be essential to ensure that environmental policies and sustainable development goals are not compromised in the wake of secessionist movements.

Additionally, the secessionist movements may exacerbate regional and global inequalities in resource distribution. Resource-rich regions seeking independence may retain control over valuable resources, potentially leading to geopolitical tensions and conflicts over access to these resources. Furthermore, the environmental impact of resource extraction and exploitation could disproportionately affect marginalized communities, exacerbating social and economic disparities.

In summary, the emergence of multiple independent states resulting from secessionist movements poses significant challenges for environmental policies and sustainable development. It is crucial for diplomats and economists to understand and address these challenges to ensure a coordinated and sustainable approach to resource management, energy security, and environmental protection. Collaboration and the establishment of international frameworks will be vital to mitigate the negative impacts and harness the opportunities presented by these secessionist movements.

Chapter 6: Minority rights: Investigating the protection of minority rights within newly independent states, addressing potential conflicts and ensuring inclusivity.

Minority rights and secessionist movements

Minority rights and secessionist movements have become increasingly significant in the modern political landscape, with various groups seeking independence and self-determination. This subchapter delves into the complex issues surrounding minority rights within newly independent states resulting from secessionist movements. Addressed to diplomats and economists, it aims to explore the protection of minority rights, potential conflicts, and ensuring inclusivity.

When secessionist movements succeed and new states emerge, one of the critical concerns is how minority rights will be safeguarded in these newly independent entities. In many cases, secessionist movements are driven by minority groups who feel marginalized and oppressed within a larger state. However, achieving independence does not automatically guarantee the protection of minority rights. The book examines the challenges and opportunities in this regard.

A comprehensive analysis of minority rights within newly independent states will involve studying various aspects. Firstly, it is important to assess the potential conflicts that may arise between the majority population and minority groups. The book explores how historical grievances, cultural differences, and power dynamics can impact the relationship between these groups and the state, and how such conflicts can be effectively managed.

Furthermore, ensuring inclusivity is crucial in order to foster peaceful coexistence and social harmony. The book discusses strategies for promoting inclusivity, such as affirmative action policies, political representation, and cultural preservation. It also examines how the international community can play a role in encouraging states to prioritize the protection of minority rights through diplomatic channels and economic incentives.

Additionally, the subchapter investigates the broader implications of minority rights within the context of secessionist movements. It explores how the protection of minority rights can contribute to regional stability, reconciliation, and the prevention of future secessionist movements. The book emphasizes the importance of addressing socioeconomic disparities, promoting equal access to resources, and ensuring the provision of social services to all citizens.

Overall, this subchapter serves as a comprehensive guide for diplomats and economists on navigating the challenges and opportunities surrounding minority rights within newly independent states resulting from secessionist movements. By addressing potential conflicts, promoting inclusivity, and examining the broader implications, it aims to contribute to the establishment of stable, inclusive, and prosperous new states.

Addressing potential conflicts and promoting inclusivity

In the wake of successful secessionist movements, it is crucial to address potential conflicts and promote inclusivity within newly independent states. This subchapter aims to shed light on the various challenges and opportunities that arise in this process, with a focus on the protection of minority rights and ensuring a harmonious coexistence among diverse populations.

One of the key concerns when multiple independent states emerge from secessionist movements is the protection of minority rights. In order to prevent social unrest and potential conflicts, it is imperative to establish mechanisms that safeguard the rights and interests of minority groups. This entails creating inclusive governance structures that reflect the diversity of the population and ensure their active participation in decision-making processes.

Furthermore, addressing potential conflicts and promoting inclusivity requires a comprehensive approach that encompasses cultural preservation. The distinct cultures within newly independent states must be recognized and celebrated, as they contribute to the richness and diversity of the global community. Efforts should be made to preserve and promote these cultures through initiatives such as language preservation, cultural education programs, and the protection of cultural heritage.

Another aspect that needs to be taken into account is socioeconomic disparities. Secessionist movements may result in widening disparities in wealth, development, and access to social services between newly independent states and their counterparts. It is crucial to address these disparities through targeted policies and investments that promote equitable development and bridge the gaps between regions.

Additionally, the establishment of new governments, legal systems, and institutions presents both challenges and opportunities. This subchapter will delve into the complexities of governance and institution-building in the aftermath of successful secessionist movements. It will explore the potential hurdles and highlight best practices in creating stable and inclusive governance structures that promote the rule of law and protect individual rights.

Lastly, the subchapter will touch upon the issue of international recognition of newly independent states. It will assess the processes and implications of international recognition, including their participation in global organizations and treaties. This aspect is crucial in ensuring the diplomatic legitimacy and stability of these states, as well as their ability to engage in global affairs.

In conclusion, addressing potential conflicts and promoting inclusivity is of paramount importance in the aftermath of successful secessionist movements. This subchapter will shed light on the challenges and opportunities associated with minority rights protection, cultural preservation, socioeconomic disparities, governance, international recognition, and their broader implications on global governance structures. By understanding these dynamics, diplomats and economists can contribute to the establishment of stable, inclusive, and prosperous newly independent states.

Legal frameworks for protecting minority rights

One of the crucial aspects to consider when exploring the consequences of secessionist movements is the protection of minority rights within newly independent states. As diplomats and economists, it is important to understand the potential conflicts that may arise and ensure inclusivity in these emerging nations.

Minority rights are fundamental to upholding the principles of democracy, human rights, and social justice. However, in the context of secessionist movements, there is a risk that minority groups may face discrimination or marginalization in the newly formed states.

To address this challenge, robust legal frameworks must be established to safeguard the rights of all individuals, regardless of their ethnicity, religion, or language. These legal frameworks should be based on international human rights standards and should include provisions for the protection of cultural, linguistic, and religious diversity.

One approach to protecting minority rights is through the adoption of comprehensive anti-discrimination legislation. Such legislation should prohibit discrimination on the basis of race, religion, ethnicity, and other relevant factors. It should also incorporate mechanisms for individuals to seek redress for any violations of their rights.

In addition to anti-discrimination laws, affirmative action policies can be implemented to promote the inclusion and representation of minority groups in various spheres of society. This can include measures such as quotas in political representation, education, and employment.

Furthermore, legal frameworks should encompass the recognition and protection of cultural rights. This includes the right to practice one's own culture, preserve cultural heritage, and participate in cultural life. Efforts should be made to ensure that minority cultures are not only protected but also promoted within the newly independent states.

To ensure the effective implementation of these legal frameworks, institutions and mechanisms for monitoring, oversight, and enforcement should be established. This can include independent human rights commissions, ombudsmen, and judicial bodies specializing in minority rights.

By prioritizing the protection of minority rights within newly independent states, diplomats and economists can contribute to the establishment of inclusive and just societies. This, in turn, can help mitigate potential conflicts and promote stability in the wake of successful secessionist movements.

Balancing majority rule and minority rights in a fragmented political landscape

In the wake of successful secessionist movements, the world is faced with a fragmented political landscape that raises important questions about the delicate balance between majority rule and minority rights. This subchapter delves into the complexities of this issue, aiming to provide valuable insights for diplomats and economists grappling with the consequences of such movements.

One of the key concerns in a fragmented political landscape is the protection of minority rights within newly independent states. As regions seek independence, there is a risk of potential conflicts arising between different ethnic, religious, or cultural groups. It is imperative to address these conflicts and ensure inclusivity, as failure to do so could lead to further instability and social unrest. This subchapter explores strategies to safeguard minority rights, such as promoting inclusive governance structures and enacting legislation that guarantees equal opportunities and protections for all citizens.

Moreover, the subchapter also examines the challenges and opportunities of establishing new governments, legal systems, and institutions in the wake of successful secessionist movements. The process of institution-building requires careful consideration to ensure that democratic principles, the rule of law, and human rights are upheld.

It also presents an opportunity to address historical grievances and create a more inclusive society.

Another aspect to be explored is the potential widening disparities in wealth, development, and social services between newly independent states and their counterparts. Economic implications of secessionist movements need to be analyzed in-depth, focusing on the impact on trade, economy, and financial systems. This subchapter investigates the potential consequences of these disparities and suggests ways to mitigate them, such as promoting economic cooperation and regional integration.

Furthermore, the subchapter also addresses the broader implications of successful secessionist movements worldwide. It examines the impact on international relations, the rise of nationalism, and the reshaping of global governance structures. The recognition of newly independent states on the international stage is a crucial aspect to consider, as it influences their participation in global organizations and treaties.

In conclusion, the subchapter "Balancing majority rule and minority rights in a fragmented political landscape" highlights the complexities and challenges of navigating the aftermath of successful secessionist movements. It offers valuable insights for diplomats and economists, providing a comprehensive analysis of the economic, political, cultural, and social dimensions that arise in a fragmented political landscape. By addressing these issues, policymakers can work towards creating a more stable, inclusive, and prosperous future for all parties involved.

Chapter 7: Governance and institution-building: Exploring the challenges and opportunities of establishing new governments, legal systems, and institutions in the wake of successful secessionist movements.

Challenges in establishing new governments and legal systems

The establishment of new governments and legal systems in the aftermath of successful secessionist movements presents a unique set of challenges and opportunities. Diplomats and economists play a pivotal role in understanding and addressing these challenges, which have far-reaching implications for various aspects of society and the global landscape. This subchapter delves into the intricacies of this process, shedding light on the following key areas:

Governance and institution-building: Creating stable and effective governments is a fundamental challenge faced by newly independent states. As diplomats and economists, understanding the complexities of institution-building is crucial. This involves establishing robust legal frameworks, responsive administrative systems, and transparent governance structures that uphold the rule of law while ensuring inclusivity and citizen participation. Addressing these challenges is vital for fostering political stability and social cohesion.

Legal systems: Developing a comprehensive legal system is essential for protecting individual rights, promoting economic growth, and ensuring social justice. Diplomats and economists must analyze the existing legal frameworks and determine whether they are suitable for the newly independent states. They must identify potential gaps and work towards establishing legal systems that are fair, efficient, and capable of addressing the needs and aspirations of the diverse population.

International recognition: Achieving international recognition for newly independent states is a critical step in their integration into the global community. Diplomats and economists must navigate the complex terrain of international relations, advocating for recognition and participation in global organizations and treaties. They must also assess the implications of recognition, including the potential impact on regional power dynamics, alliances, and diplomatic relations.

Minority rights: Protecting minority rights is a key aspect of ensuring inclusivity and social harmony within newly independent states. Diplomats and economists must be cognizant of potential conflicts arising from ethnic or religious differences and work towards promoting understanding, tolerance, and equality. They must advocate for policies that safeguard minority rights and foster a sense of belonging and participation for all citizens.

Socioeconomic disparities: The emergence of newly independent states from secessionist movements can lead to widening disparities in wealth, development, and social services. Diplomats and economists must analyze the potential economic implications of such disparities and work towards mitigating them. This involves formulating policies that promote equitable resource distribution, encourage economic growth, and bridge the gaps between the newly independent states and their counterparts.

In conclusion, establishing new governments and legal systems in the wake of successful secessionist movements poses a myriad of challenges. Diplomats and economists must grapple with issues related to governance, legal systems, international recognition, minority rights, and socioeconomic disparities. By addressing these challenges head-on, they can contribute to the stability, inclusivity, and prosperity of newly independent states, while also shaping the broader global landscape.

Institution-building and capacity development

Institution-building and capacity development play a crucial role in the aftermath of successful secessionist movements. The establishment of new governments, legal systems, and institutions becomes essential to navigate the challenges and opportunities that arise in newly independent states. This subchapter will delve into the various aspects of governance and institution-building in the wake of secessionist movements, addressing the concerns of diplomats and economists.

One of the primary challenges in institution-building is the creation of a stable political framework that ensures inclusive governance. The book will explore the ways in which new governments can address potential conflicts and protect minority rights within their territories. It will analyze the strategies employed to maintain social cohesion and foster inclusivity, considering the potential for socioeconomic disparities between newly independent states and their counterparts.

The subchapter will also examine the economic implications of secessionist movements. It will analyze the impact on trade, economy, and financial systems if all secessionist movements were successful in achieving independence. This will involve a comprehensive assessment of the potential consequences for global resource distribution, energy security, and environmental policies, particularly in resource-rich regions seeking independence.

Furthermore, the book will address the diplomatic consequences of multiple independent states emerging from secessionist movements. It will explore the potential effects on diplomatic relations, alliances, and regional power dynamics. The subchapter will assess the processes and implications of international recognition of newly independent states, including their participation in global organizations and treaties. This analysis will shed light on the broader implications of successful secessionist movements worldwide, such as the impact on international relations, the rise of nationalism, and the reshaping of global governance structures.

Lastly, the subchapter will highlight the importance of cultural preservation within newly independent states resulting from secessionist movements. It will examine strategies to promote and protect distinct cultures, ensuring their preservation in the face of globalization and homogenization.

Overall, this subchapter on institution-building and capacity development will provide diplomats and economists with a comprehensive understanding of the challenges and opportunities that emerge after successful secessionist movements. It will shed light on the intricate dynamics of governance, economics, diplomacy, and culture in these newly independent states, contributing to a holistic understanding of the aftermath of secessionist movements.

Transitional justice and reconciliation processes

Transitional justice and reconciliation processes play a crucial role in the aftermath of successful secessionist movements, as they address the challenges of healing divisions, fostering harmony, and ensuring a just and equitable future for all. This subchapter explores the significance of transitional justice and reconciliation processes in the context of political fragmentation resulting from secessionist movements.

In the wake of successful secessionist movements, the need for transitional justice mechanisms becomes paramount. These processes aim to address past human rights abuses, promote accountability, and provide redress for victims. Diplomats and economists must recognize the economic implications of transitional justice, as it can have a significant impact on trade, investment, and financial systems. Reconciliation processes are equally important, as they facilitate the building of trust and social cohesion between different communities within newly independent states.

Additionally, transitional justice and reconciliation processes have significant political implications. They can shape diplomatic relations, alliances, and regional power dynamics. Diplomats and economists need to understand the potential consequences of multiple independent states emerging from secessionist movements, including the challenges of negotiating new diplomatic relationships and balancing regional interests.

Cultural preservation is another critical aspect that needs attention in the aftermath of secessionist movements. Newly independent states must focus on preserving and promoting their distinct cultures, ensuring the protection of minority rights and fostering inclusivity. Failure to address cultural preservation can lead to social unrest and exacerbate divisions within society.

Furthermore, transitional justice and reconciliation processes must tackle national security challenges arising from multiple independent states. Diplomats and economists should analyze the security implications, such as border disputes, defense alliances, and regional stability, to ensure peaceful coexistence and prevent conflicts.

Resource management is another key consideration. Successful secessionist movements in resource-rich regions can impact global resource distribution, energy security, and environmental policies. Diplomats and economists must analyze the consequences to ensure sustainable development and equitable resource allocation.

Governance and institution-building are fundamental in the aftermath of secessionist movements. Diplomats and economists need to explore the challenges and opportunities of establishing new governments, legal systems, and institutions to ensure stability, justice, and effective governance.

International recognition of newly independent states is a crucial process that diplomats and economists must assess. The implications of international recognition, including participation in global organizations and treaties, can shape the trajectory of these states and their relations with the international community.

Socioeconomic disparities can emerge between newly independent states and their counterparts, posing challenges for development and social services. Diplomats and economists must investigate these potential disparities and work towards bridging the gap to ensure equitable growth.

Lastly, secessionist movements as a global trend have broader implications for international relations, the rise of nationalism, and the reshaping of global governance structures. Diplomats and economists must analyze these trends and their impact on the global order.

In conclusion, transitional justice and reconciliation processes are essential in addressing the challenges and opportunities that arise from successful secessionist movements. Diplomats and economists must recognize the various dimensions of these processes, including their economic implications, political consequences, cultural preservation, national security challenges, resource management, minority rights, governance and institution-building, international recognition, socioeconomic disparities, and the global trend of secessionist movements. By understanding and addressing these issues, diplomats and economists can contribute to a peaceful and prosperous future for newly independent states and the international community as a whole.

Strengthening governance in a fragmented political landscape

In the rapidly changing world of politics, the rise of secessionist movements presents a unique challenge to diplomats and economists. The subchapter titled "Strengthening Governance in a Fragmented Political Landscape" delves into the crucial task of establishing robust governance structures in newly independent states resulting from secessionist movements. This chapter aims to guide diplomats and economists in understanding the challenges and opportunities that arise in this complex scenario.

The successful achievement of independence by secessionist movements has significant implications for various aspects of governance and institution-building. The establishment of new governments, legal systems, and institutions becomes imperative to ensure stability, inclusivity, and effective governance. This subchapter explores the challenges faced in this process and identifies potential opportunities for innovation and development.

One of the primary concerns in this fragmented political landscape is the preservation and promotion of distinct cultures within newly independent states. The chapter emphasizes the importance of cultural preservation and provides insights into strategies that can be employed to protect minority cultures and promote inclusivity. It also addresses potential conflicts that may arise and suggests ways to ensure cultural harmony.

Furthermore, the subchapter sheds light on the economic implications of secessionist movements. It analyzes the impact on trade, economy, and financial systems if all secessionist movements were successful in achieving independence. By examining the potential consequences of multiple independent states emerging, including diplomatic relations, alliances, and regional power dynamics, diplomats and economists can gain a comprehensive understanding of the economic landscape in this fragmented political scenario.

Additionally, the chapter explores the national security challenges arising from multiple independent states. It examines border disputes, defense alliances, and regional stability, providing policymakers with insights into potential conflicts and suggesting strategies for managing security concerns.

Resource management is another critical aspect discussed in this subchapter. It analyzes how resource-rich regions seeking independence could impact global resource distribution, energy security, and environmental policies. By understanding the implications of these movements on resource management, diplomats and economists can develop strategies to ensure sustainable development and global resource stability.

Lastly, the subchapter assesses the processes and implications of international recognition of newly independent states. It explores their participation in global organizations and treaties, shedding light on the diplomatic dimensions of secessionist movements.

In conclusion, "Strengthening Governance in a Fragmented Political Landscape" is a comprehensive subchapter that addresses the multifaceted challenges and opportunities presented by secessionist movements. By focusing on governance and institution-building, cultural preservation, economic implications, national security challenges, resource management, minority rights, international recognition, socioeconomic disparities, and the broader implications of secessionist movements as a global trend, diplomats and economists can navigate this complex landscape with greater insight and effectiveness.

Chapter 8: International recognition: Assessing the processes and implications of international recognition of newly independent states, including their participation in global organizations and treaties.

Processes and criteria for international recognition

In the complex and rapidly evolving landscape of secessionist movements, understanding the processes and criteria for international recognition is crucial for diplomats and economists alike. This subchapter explores the intricacies of this topic, shedding light on the implications and challenges associated with the recognition of newly independent states.

At the heart of the matter lies the question of how a secessionist movement can achieve international recognition. While the recognition of a new state ultimately rests on the political will of existing sovereign states, there are certain criteria and processes that can influence this decision-making process.

First and foremost, diplomats and economists must delve into the economic implications of recognizing a new state. Analyzing the impact on trade, economy, and financial systems is vital in order to grasp the potential consequences for both the seceding region and the international community. Understanding the economic viability and potential risks is crucial in determining whether recognition is warranted.

Political fragmentation is another critical aspect to consider. The emergence of multiple independent states from secessionist movements can have far-reaching consequences for diplomatic relations, alliances, and regional power dynamics. Diplomats must navigate this complex web of relationships and understand the potential changes in the geopolitical landscape.

Cultural preservation is also a significant consideration. Focusing on the preservation and promotion of distinct cultures within newly independent states resulting from secessionist movements is essential to ensure inclusivity and avoid cultural assimilation. Protecting minority rights and addressing potential conflicts is crucial in fostering a harmonious and diverse society.

National security challenges cannot be overlooked. The security implications of multiple independent states emerging must be thoroughly examined, including border disputes, defense alliances, and regional stability. Diplomats must work to mitigate potential conflicts and ensure the security of all parties involved.

Resource management is yet another critical area of concern. Analyzing how resource-rich regions seeking independence could impact global resource distribution, energy security, and environmental policies is crucial in order to develop sustainable solutions and avoid resource conflicts.

Governance and institution-building are paramount in the aftermath of successful secessionist movements. Exploring the challenges and opportunities of establishing new governments, legal systems, and institutions is vital in ensuring effective governance and stability.

The process of international recognition itself must also be assessed. Diplomats and economists must examine the processes and implications of international recognition, including the newly independent state's participation in global organizations and treaties.

Socioeconomic disparities are a potential consequence of secessionist movements. Investigating the potential for widening disparities in wealth, development, and social services between newly independent states and their counterparts is crucial in order to address these disparities and promote equitable development.

Lastly, secessionist movements as a global trend must be examined in a broader context. This includes investigating the impact on international relations, the rise of nationalism, and the reshaping of global governance structures. Understanding the global implications of successful secessionist movements is key to navigating this evolving landscape.

In conclusion, understanding the processes and criteria for international recognition is essential for diplomats and economists grappling with the consequences of secessionist movements. By analyzing the economic, political, cultural, security, resource, governance, socioeconomic, and global implications, we can gain valuable insights into this complex phenomenon and work towards promoting stability, inclusivity, and sustainable development in the wake of successful secessionist movements.

Implications for global organizations and treaties

The successful achievement of independence by secessionist movements holds significant implications for global organizations and treaties. Diplomats and economists must closely examine these implications to fully understand the potential consequences and challenges that may arise from such political fragmentation.

Economic implications are a crucial aspect to consider. The impact on trade, economy, and financial systems would be substantial if all secessionist movements were successful in attaining independence. The disruption of established economic structures and the introduction of new currencies and regulations would require careful analysis and planning. Furthermore, the potential loss or gain of economic partners and markets would significantly affect global trade dynamics and investment patterns.

Political fragmentation resulting from multiple independent states emerging from secessionist movements raises questions about the future of diplomatic relations, alliances, and regional power dynamics. Diplomats need to assess how these newly formed states would navigate their relationships with neighboring countries, regional organizations, and international bodies. The balance of power in a region could shift, leading to potential conflicts or alliances.

Cultural preservation is another important consideration. The promotion and preservation of distinct cultures within newly independent states resulting from secessionist movements must be addressed. Diplomats and economists need to examine how these states can maintain their cultural identity while engaging with the global community. Cultural diversity should be celebrated, but efforts must be made to ensure inclusivity and avoid potential conflicts arising from cultural differences.

National security challenges are a crucial aspect to analyze. Multiple independent states emerging from secessionist movements could lead to border disputes, defense alliances, and regional stability concerns. Diplomats must evaluate the impact on regional security dynamics and work towards maintaining stability and peace.

Resource management is another critical aspect to investigate. Resource-rich regions seeking independence could impact global resource distribution, energy security, and environmental policies. Diplomats and economists need to assess how these changes would affect global markets, energy supply chains, and environmental sustainability efforts.

Minority rights within newly independent states must be protected to avoid potential conflicts and ensure inclusivity. Diplomats and economists have a responsibility to address the challenges of safeguarding minority rights and promoting social cohesion within these new states.

The establishment of new governments, legal systems, and institutions is a significant challenge and opportunity that arises from successful secessionist movements. Diplomats and economists must explore the potential pitfalls and benefits of governance and institution-building in these newly independent states.

International recognition of newly independent states is a crucial aspect to assess. Diplomats need to evaluate the processes and implications of international recognition, including their participation in global organizations and treaties. The recognition of these states could reshape global governance structures and international relations.

Socioeconomic disparities between newly independent states and their counterparts must be investigated. Diplomats and economists need to analyze the potential for widening disparities in wealth, development, and social services. Efforts should be made to bridge these gaps and ensure that all states have equal opportunities for growth and development.

Examining successful secessionist movements as a global trend is essential. Diplomats and economists must analyze the broader implications of these movements worldwide, including the impact on international relations, the rise of nationalism, and the reshaping of global governance structures. Understanding this trend is crucial for developing effective policies and strategies to address the challenges and opportunities it presents.

Diplomatic efforts and international legitimacy

In the complex and ever-evolving landscape of secessionist movements, the diplomatic efforts undertaken by aspiring independent states play a crucial role in determining their international legitimacy. This subchapter delves into the multifaceted aspects of diplomatic engagement and the subsequent implications for global governance structures.

For diplomats and economists, understanding the economic implications of successful secessionist movements is of paramount importance. Analyzing the impact on trade, economy, and financial systems if all secessionist movements were successful in achieving independence sheds light on the potential disruptions and opportunities that arise. The intricate web of economic interdependencies and the need for new trade agreements, currency arrangements, and market access are key considerations for diplomats and economists alike.

Moreover, the political fragmentation resulting from multiple independent states emerging from secessionist movements presents a myriad of challenges. Diplomatic relations, alliances, and regional power dynamics undergo significant transformations. The subchapter explores the potential consequences of such fragmentation, providing insights into the reshaping of international alliances and the diplomacy required to navigate these new geopolitical landscapes.

Cultural preservation within newly independent states is another crucial aspect that warrants attention. As secessionist movements often aim to protect and promote distinctive cultures, diplomats must address the challenges of preserving cultural heritage while fostering inclusivity and diversity. Finding a delicate balance between cultural promotion and minority rights is a task that requires diplomatic finesse and sensitivity.

National security challenges are inevitable when multiple independent states emerge. This subchapter examines the security implications, including border disputes, defense alliances, and regional stability. Diplomats and economists must grapple with the complexities of ensuring security cooperation, managing potential conflicts, and forging new defense alliances that safeguard the interests of all parties involved.

Resource management is yet another critical area that demands analysis. The impact of resource-rich regions seeking independence on global resource distribution, energy security, and environmental policies cannot be underestimated. Diplomats and economists must assess and navigate the potential disruptions and opportunities arising from these circumstances.

Additionally, the subchapter delves into minority rights within newly independent states, addressing potential conflicts and ensuring inclusivity. It explores the challenges and opportunities of establishing new governments, legal systems, and institutions in the wake of successful secessionist movements. Diplomats and economists play a pivotal role in facilitating inclusive governance and institution-building processes.

International recognition of newly independent states is a key aspect that impacts their participation in global organizations and treaties.

Examining the processes and implications of international recognition sheds light on the diplomatic efforts required to gain legitimacy on the international stage.

Lastly, the subchapter investigates the broader implications of successful secessionist movements worldwide. This includes the impact on international relations, the rise of nationalism, and the reshaping of global governance structures. Understanding secessionist movements as a global trend is crucial for diplomats and economists in comprehending the far-reaching consequences and shaping effective diplomatic strategies.

In conclusion, the subchapter on diplomatic efforts and international legitimacy provides diplomats and economists with a comprehensive understanding of the intricacies and implications of secessionist movements. From economic implications and political fragmentation to cultural preservation and resource management, this subchapter equips its readers with the knowledge and insights needed to navigate the complex world of secessionist movements and their diplomatic consequences.

Balancing sovereignty and international cooperation in a fragmented political landscape

In the current global political landscape, secessionist movements are gaining momentum, posing significant challenges to the balance between sovereignty and international cooperation. This subchapter delves deep into the intricate web of diplomatic consequences that arise from such movements, addressing diplomats and economists who seek to understand the multifaceted dimensions of this complex issue.

One of the primary concerns explored in this subchapter is the economic implications of successful secessionist movements. By analyzing the impact on trade, economy, and financial systems, we aim to shed light on the potential consequences of multiple independent states emerging from secessionist movements. This includes examining the disruptions in established trade relationships, the volatility in financial markets, and the challenges in maintaining economic stability.

Further, we delve into the political fragmentation resulting from these movements, exploring the potential consequences on diplomatic relations, alliances, and regional power dynamics. We assess the challenges of establishing diplomatic ties with newly independent states, the realignment of alliances, and the potential for power shifts in regional and global politics.

Cultural preservation is another critical aspect addressed in this subchapter. We examine the preservation and promotion of distinct cultures within newly independent states, considering the need to safeguard cultural heritage while fostering inclusivity and social harmony.

The subchapter also delves into the national security challenges arising from multiple independent states emerging. We analyze the potential for border disputes, the complexities of defense alliances, and the impact on regional stability. Understanding these security implications is vital in developing effective strategies to maintain peace and stability in a fragmented political landscape.

Additionally, we explore the impact of resource-rich regions seeking independence on global resource distribution, energy security, and environmental policies. By analyzing these resource management challenges, we offer insights into potential disruptions and the need for sustainable policies.

The protection of minority rights within newly independent states is another critical concern addressed in this subchapter. We investigate potential conflicts and present strategies to ensure inclusivity and equitable representation of minority groups in the newly established states.

Governance and institution-building are also examined, focusing on the challenges and opportunities of establishing new governments, legal systems, and institutions. This analysis will aid in understanding the processes involved in successful institution-building following secessionist movements.

International recognition of newly independent states is also a crucial aspect explored. We assess the processes and implications of international recognition, including their participation in global organizations and treaties. Understanding the dynamics of international recognition helps in comprehending the evolving nature of global governance structures.

Lastly, we explore the potential widening of socioeconomic disparities between newly independent states and their counterparts. This investigation aids in identifying the challenges in achieving equitable development and social services amidst political fragmentation.

By examining secessionist movements as a global trend, this subchapter sheds light on the broader implications for international relations, the rise of nationalism, and the reshaping of global governance structures. It serves as a comprehensive resource for diplomats and economists seeking a nuanced understanding of the diplomatic consequences of secessionist movements in today's fragmented political landscape.

Chapter 9: Socioeconomic disparities: Investigating the potential for widening disparities in wealth, development, and social services between newly independent states and their counterparts.

Economic disparities and development challenges

In the realm of secessionist movements, the economic implications are vast and far-reaching. The successful achievement of independence by various regions poses a number of challenges and opportunities for both trade and economy, as well as the financial systems of the newly independent states and their counterparts. This subchapter aims to analyze the potential impact on these aspects if secessionist movements were to triumph.

One of the primary concerns is the effect on trade. With the emergence of multiple independent states, trade dynamics would undergo significant changes. The establishment of new borders and the need to renegotiate trade agreements would disrupt existing trade patterns, potentially leading to economic instability. Diplomats and economists need to closely examine the potential consequences of these changes and explore strategies to mitigate adverse effects.

Furthermore, the political fragmentation resulting from secessionist movements raises important questions about diplomatic relations, alliances, and regional power dynamics. The emergence of multiple independent states could lead to shifts in alliances and the redistribution of political power, which can have both positive and negative consequences on regional stability and international relations. Understanding these potential consequences is crucial for diplomats and economists in order to navigate the evolving diplomatic landscape effectively.

Additionally, cultural preservation is a critical aspect that must be considered when analyzing the impact of secessionist movements. Newly independent states may prioritize the preservation and promotion of their distinct cultures, which could lead to challenges in terms of inclusivity and minority rights. Diplomats and economists should explore ways to address potential conflicts and ensure that the newly independent states are inclusive and respectful of minority rights.

The resource management aspect of secessionist movements is also of great significance. Resource-rich regions seeking independence could disrupt global resource distribution, impact energy security, and influence environmental policies. By analyzing the potential consequences of this scenario, diplomats and economists can work towards solutions that ensure equitable resource distribution, sustainable energy practices, and environmental protection.

Lastly, the subchapter will explore the socioeconomic disparities that may arise between newly independent states and their counterparts. The successful achievement of independence could widen the disparities in wealth, development, and social services, potentially leading to regional imbalances and social unrest. Diplomats and economists need to investigate strategies to address these disparities and promote inclusive and sustainable development.

In conclusion, the economic disparities and development challenges resulting from secessionist movements are wide-ranging and complex. Diplomats and economists must carefully analyze the potential impact on trade, economy, and financial systems, as well as consider the broader implications on diplomatic relations, cultural preservation, national security, resource management, minority rights, governance, and international recognition. By understanding these challenges, policymakers can work towards creating a more stable, inclusive, and prosperous world in the face of increasing secessionist movements.

Social service provision and welfare systems

Social service provision and welfare systems play a crucial role in the aftermath of successful secessionist movements. As diplomats and economists, it is crucial to analyze the implications of social service provision and welfare systems in the context of various secessionist movements and their potential consequences.

One of the key economic implications of successful secessionist movements is the impact on trade, economy, and financial systems. With multiple independent states emerging, there may be disruptions in trade relations and economic integration. Diplomats and economists must closely examine the potential challenges and opportunities in establishing new economic frameworks and trade agreements to ensure the continued prosperity of all parties involved.

Moreover, the emergence of multiple independent states can have significant political ramifications, including diplomatic relations, alliances, and regional power dynamics. It is important to explore how these new states will navigate their diplomatic relationships and establish alliances, as well as the potential shifts in regional power dynamics that may occur. This will require careful analysis and strategic decision-making to maintain stability and peace in the region.

Cultural preservation is another critical aspect to consider within newly independent states resulting from secessionist movements. Diplomats and economists should focus on promoting and preserving distinct cultures, ensuring that minority cultures are protected and celebrated. This includes supporting initiatives that promote cultural diversity and inclusivity, while also addressing any potential conflicts that may arise.

National security challenges are also a crucial consideration when analyzing the implications of secessionist movements. Border disputes, defense alliances, and regional stability can all be affected by the emergence of multiple independent states. Diplomats and economists must carefully examine and address these challenges to prevent potential conflicts and ensure the security of all parties involved.

Resource management is another important factor to consider. Resource-rich regions seeking independence can significantly impact global resource distribution, energy security, and environmental policies. It is essential to assess the potential consequences of such movements and develop sustainable resource management strategies that prioritize global cooperation and environmental conservation.

Furthermore, the protection of minority rights within newly independent states is of utmost importance. Inclusivity and addressing potential conflicts should be a priority to ensure the rights and well-being of all individuals in these states.

Governance and institution-building present both challenges and opportunities in the wake of successful secessionist movements. Establishing new governments, legal systems, and institutions requires careful planning and strategic thinking to ensure stability and effective governance.

The processes and implications of international recognition of newly independent states must also be assessed. This includes their participation in global organizations and treaties, as well as their role in global governance structures.

Socioeconomic disparities may arise between newly independent states and their counterparts. Diplomats and economists should investigate the potential for widening disparities in wealth, development, and social services, and work towards mitigating these disparities through inclusive policies and economic cooperation.

Finally, it is crucial to examine the broader implications of successful secessionist movements worldwide. This includes the impact on international relations, the rise of nationalism, and the reshaping of global governance structures. Understanding these implications can inform diplomatic and economic strategies to address the challenges and opportunities presented by secessionist movements globally.

In conclusion, the subchapter on social service provision and welfare systems in the book "Political Fragmentation: The Diplomatic Consequences of Secessionist Movements" provides a comprehensive analysis of the implications of successful secessionist movements. It addresses the economic, political, cultural, security, resource management, minority rights, governance, international recognition, socioeconomic disparities, and global trend aspects, offering valuable insights for diplomats and economists navigating the complex landscape of secessionist movements.

Reducing socioeconomic disparities in a fragmented political landscape

In a world where secessionist movements are increasingly gaining traction, it is imperative to address the potential consequences of political fragmentation on socioeconomic disparities. This subchapter delves into the challenges of reducing such disparities in a fragmented political landscape, with a focus on the implications for diplomats and economists.

The successful achievement of independence by secessionist movements has the potential to disrupt trade, economy, and financial systems. As new independent states emerge, it is crucial to analyze the impact on global trade dynamics, economic growth, and financial stability. Diplomats and economists must collaborate to develop strategies that minimize disruptions and ensure the smooth functioning of international economic systems.

Political fragmentation resulting from secessionist movements also has significant implications for diplomatic relations, alliances, and regional power dynamics. Diplomats play a pivotal role in managing these consequences, fostering dialogue, and finding common ground among newly independent states to maintain stability and prevent conflicts. Economists, on the other hand, can assess the economic implications of these changes, such as the redistribution of resources and the potential for economic cooperation among independent states.

Cultural preservation is another crucial aspect to consider in the wake of successful secessionist movements. Diplomats and economists must work together to promote the preservation and promotion of distinct cultures within newly independent states. This includes supporting cultural initiatives, preserving heritage sites, and ensuring the inclusivity of minority cultures.

Socioeconomic disparities can arise between newly independent states and their counterparts, leading to issues of wealth inequality, uneven development, and limited access to social services. Diplomats and economists must prioritize addressing these disparities through targeted policies, investment in infrastructure, and capacity-building initiatives. Collaborative efforts can contribute to narrowing the gap and ensuring a more equitable distribution of resources and opportunities.

Additionally, governance and institution-building in the aftermath of successful secessionist movements pose significant challenges. Diplomats and economists can provide guidance and expertise in establishing new governments, legal systems, and institutions that uphold democratic values, promote transparency, and ensure effective governance.

International recognition is a crucial factor in the success and stability of newly independent states. Diplomats and economists can analyze the processes and implications of international recognition, including the participation of these states in global organizations and treaties. Ensuring their integration into the international community can contribute to their economic development and overall stability.

In conclusion, reducing socioeconomic disparities in a fragmented political landscape requires close collaboration between diplomats and economists. By addressing the economic implications, political consequences, cultural preservation, minority rights, governance challenges, international recognition, and resource management, these professionals can contribute to creating a more inclusive, stable, and equitable global landscape in the face of secessionist movements.

Promoting inclusive growth and equitable development

Promoting inclusive growth and equitable development is a crucial aspect to consider when analyzing the impact of secessionist movements on trade, economy, and financial systems. Diplomats and economists need to assess the economic implications of successful secessionist movements and the potential consequences of multiple independent states emerging from such movements.

From an economic perspective, the fragmentation caused by secessionist movements can lead to disruptions in trade and economic activities. The separation of regions from larger states could result in the formation of new borders, customs regulations, and trade barriers. Diplomats and economists must carefully analyze how these changes may affect the flow of goods, services, and investments, and devise strategies to mitigate potential negative impacts.

Moreover, the emergence of multiple independent states can also have significant implications for the financial systems of the affected regions. Diplomats and economists should evaluate the potential challenges of establishing new currencies, banking systems, and monetary policies. They must also consider the impact on foreign investments, debt obligations, and international financial institutions.

In addition to economic considerations, promoting inclusive growth and equitable development requires addressing cultural preservation within newly independent states resulting from secessionist movements. Diplomats and economists should prioritize the protection and promotion of distinct cultures, languages, and traditions. This can be achieved through policies that support cultural institutions, educational programs, and the preservation of historical sites.

Furthermore, diplomats and economists need to examine the national security challenges arising from multiple independent states. Border disputes, defense alliances, and regional stability should be carefully assessed to prevent potential conflicts and ensure the security of all parties involved.

Resource management is another critical aspect to consider. The secession of resource-rich regions can have significant implications for global resource distribution, energy security, and environmental policies. Diplomats and economists should analyze how the independence of these regions may impact the availability and prices of vital resources, as well as devise strategies to ensure sustainable resource management and energy security.

Additionally, the protection of minority rights within newly independent states is paramount. Diplomats and economists must investigate potential conflicts and ensure inclusivity for all ethnic, religious, and linguistic groups. This can be achieved through the implementation of robust legal frameworks and policies that safeguard minority rights and promote social cohesion.

Governance and institution-building are also crucial considerations. Diplomats and economists need to explore the challenges and opportunities of establishing new governments, legal systems, and institutions. They should provide guidance on effective governance, transparent institutions, and the rule of law to ensure stability and promote socio-economic development.

Another essential aspect is international recognition of newly independent states. Diplomats and economists should assess the processes and implications of international recognition, including the participation of these states in global organizations and treaties. This recognition plays a significant role in shaping diplomatic relations, alliances, and regional power dynamics.

Moreover, diplomats and economists should investigate the potential for widening disparities in wealth, development, and social services between newly independent states and their counterparts. They need to identify strategies to bridge these gaps and promote inclusive growth, ensuring that the benefits of independence are shared equitably among all citizens.

Finally, examining secessionist movements as a global trend is crucial. Diplomats and economists must analyze the broader implications of successful secessionist movements worldwide. This includes assessing the impact on international relations, the rise of nationalism, and the reshaping of global governance structures. Understanding these trends is essential for diplomats and economists to effectively navigate the evolving geopolitical landscape.

In conclusion, promoting inclusive growth and equitable development is of utmost importance when analyzing the consequences of secessionist movements. Diplomats and economists must consider the economic, political, cultural, and social aspects involved to ensure a comprehensive understanding of the implications and devise strategies to address the challenges and opportunities arising from successful secessionist movements.

Chapter 10: Secessionist movements as a global trend: Examining the broader implications of successful secessionist movements worldwide, including the impact on international relations, the rise of nationalism, and the reshaping of global governance structures.

Global trends in secessionist movements

Secessionist movements have become a prominent global trend in recent years, challenging the existing political and economic order. This subchapter aims to provide diplomats and economists with a comprehensive analysis of the various aspects and consequences of this growing phenomenon.

One of the key areas of concern is the economic implications of successful secessionist movements. Analyzing the impact on trade, economy, and financial systems if all secessionist movements were to achieve independence is crucial. The potential disruption in supply chains, changes in trade agreements, and the reconfiguration of economic structures could have far-reaching consequences for both the newly independent states and their former counterparts.

Another important aspect to consider is the political fragmentation that arises from multiple independent states emerging out of secessionist movements. This entails exploring the potential consequences for diplomatic relations, alliances, and regional power dynamics. The establishment of new diplomatic ties, renegotiation of existing alliances, and shifts in regional power balances can significantly reshape the global political landscape.

Cultural preservation is also a critical issue that needs to be addressed in the context of secessionist movements. Focusing on the preservation and promotion of distinct cultures within newly independent states is necessary to ensure inclusivity and prevent cultural assimilation. Striking a balance between cultural preservation and the formation of a cohesive national identity is a complex challenge that requires careful consideration.

The security implications of secessionist movements cannot be overlooked. Examining the potential border disputes, defense alliances, and regional stability concerns that arise from the emergence of multiple independent states is essential. Addressing these challenges requires proactive diplomacy and the establishment of mutually beneficial security arrangements.

Resource management is another significant aspect to be analyzed. Understanding how resource-rich regions seeking independence could impact global resource distribution, energy security, and environmental policies is crucial. Balancing the needs and interests of newly independent states with global resource management goals is a complex task that requires international cooperation.

Furthermore, it is essential to investigate the protection of minority rights within newly independent states. Addressing potential conflicts and ensuring inclusivity are vital in order to prevent discrimination and social unrest.

Governance and institution-building pose significant challenges and opportunities in the wake of successful secessionist movements. Establishing new governments, legal systems, and institutions requires careful planning and coordination to ensure stability and effective governance.

The subchapter also explores the processes and implications of international recognition of newly independent states. Assessing their participation in global organizations and treaties is critical for understanding the extent to which their independence is recognized and their role in global governance structures.

Socioeconomic disparities between newly independent states and their counterparts are likely to emerge. Investigating the potential for widening disparities in wealth, development, and social services is crucial. Addressing these disparities through targeted policies and international cooperation is necessary to promote sustainable development and social cohesion.

Finally, the subchapter examines secessionist movements as a global trend and the broader implications they have on international relations, the rise of nationalism, and the reshaping of global governance structures. Understanding the underlying factors driving these movements and their implications for the global order is essential for diplomats and economists alike.

In conclusion, this subchapter provides a comprehensive analysis of the global trends in secessionist movements. It addresses various niches, including economic implications, political fragmentation, cultural preservation, national security challenges, resource management, minority rights, governance and institution-building, international recognition, socioeconomic disparities, and the broader implications of this phenomenon. By considering these aspects, diplomats and economists can gain valuable insights into the complex and multifaceted nature of secessionist movements and their diplomatic consequences.

Impact on international relations and global governance

The phenomenon of secessionist movements can have far-reaching implications for international relations and global governance. This subchapter aims to explore the various dimensions of this impact, addressing the concerns of diplomats and economists. By delving into the economic, political, cultural, security, resource management, minority rights, governance, international recognition, socioeconomic disparities, and global trends aspects, we can gain a comprehensive understanding of the consequences of secessionist movements on international relations and global governance.

One of the key areas of concern is the economic implications of successful secessionist movements. This section analyzes the impact on trade, economy, and financial systems if all secessionist movements were successful in achieving independence. It assesses the potential disruptions to existing trade networks and the challenges in establishing new economic ties between the newly independent states and their counterparts.

The political fragmentation resulting from secessionist movements has diplomatic repercussions as well. This subchapter explores the potential consequences of multiple independent states emerging, including the reshuffling of diplomatic relations, alliances, and regional power dynamics. It examines the challenges in maintaining regional stability and the potential for conflicts arising from border disputes and defense alliances.

Cultural preservation is another critical aspect addressed in this subchapter. It focuses on the preservation and promotion of distinct cultures within newly independent states resulting from secessionist movements. It investigates the protection of minority rights, addressing potential conflicts and ensuring inclusivity in the newly formed nations.

The security implications of multiple independent states emerging from secessionist movements are also examined. This section delves into the potential challenges in border management, defense alliances, and regional stability. It analyzes the impact on national security and the need for collaborative efforts to maintain peace and security in the region.

Additionally, this subchapter analyzes the impact on resource management and its global implications. It assesses how resource-rich regions seeking independence could impact global resource distribution, energy security, and environmental policies. It explores the need for sustainable resource management and the potential conflicts that may arise in this context.

Furthermore, the challenges and opportunities of establishing new governments, legal systems, and institutions in the wake of successful secessionist movements are explored. This section examines the governance and institution-building process, addressing the complexities and potential pitfalls involved.

The subchapter also assesses the processes and implications of international recognition of newly independent states. It explores their participation in global organizations and treaties, as well as the diplomatic dynamics of recognition and non-recognition.

Lastly, the broader implications of successful secessionist movements worldwide are examined. This section discusses the rise of nationalism, the reshaping of global governance structures, and the impact on international relations as a whole.

By addressing these various dimensions, this subchapter provides diplomats and economists with a comprehensive analysis of the impact of secessionist movements on international relations and global governance. It equips them with the necessary knowledge to navigate the complex challenges and opportunities that arise from this phenomenon.

Rise of nationalism and its consequences

Nationalism has emerged as a powerful force in today's world, with secessionist movements gaining momentum across the globe. This subchapter delves into the consequences of this rise of nationalism, addressing a wide range of issues pertinent to diplomats and economists.

One of the key aspects explored in this subchapter is the economic implications of successful secessionist movements. By analyzing the impact on trade, economy, and financial systems, diplomats and economists can gain insights into the potential consequences of multiple independent states emerging from secessionist movements. This includes assessing the effects on regional trade dynamics, currency stability, and investment patterns.

Furthermore, political fragmentation resulting from secessionist movements has significant ramifications for diplomatic relations, alliances, and regional power dynamics. Diplomats need to understand the potential consequences of multiple independent states emerging and the challenges it poses to maintaining stability and cooperation. The subchapter examines the potential diplomatic challenges and opportunities that arise from such fragmentation.

Cultural preservation is another crucial aspect addressed in this subchapter. With the emergence of new independent states, the preservation and promotion of distinct cultures become paramount. Diplomats and economists need to explore strategies to ensure that the rights and identities of minority groups within these states are protected and that inclusivity is fostered.

The rise of nationalism and the subsequent fragmentation also brings forth national security challenges. This includes border disputes, defense alliances, and regional stability. Diplomats and economists must analyze the security implications of multiple independent states emerging and work towards mitigating potential conflicts and ensuring stability in the region.

Resource management is a critical factor to consider when examining secessionist movements. The subchapter delves into how resource-rich regions seeking independence could impact global resource distribution, energy security, and environmental policies. Diplomats and economists must assess the potential consequences and work towards developing sustainable resource management strategies.

Governance and institution-building also pose significant challenges in the wake of successful secessionist movements. Diplomats and economists need to explore the opportunities and obstacles in establishing new governments, legal systems, and institutions to ensure stability and effective governance in newly independent states.

International recognition of newly independent states is another crucial aspect examined in this subchapter. Diplomats and economists must assess the processes and implications of international recognition, including their participation in global organizations and treaties.

Finally, the subchapter investigates the potential socio-economic disparities between newly independent states and their counterparts.

Diplomats and economists need to investigate the potential widening of disparities in wealth, development, and social services and work towards ensuring inclusive and equitable growth.

In conclusion, the rise of nationalism and subsequent secessionist movements have far-reaching consequences for diplomats and economists. By analyzing the various dimensions of these movements, including economic, political, cultural, and security aspects, diplomats and economists can develop strategies to navigate the challenges and opportunities presented by this global trend.

Reshaping global governance structures in a fragmented political landscape

In today's rapidly changing political landscape, the rise of secessionist movements has become a prominent global trend. The consequences of these movements extend far beyond the borders of the newly independent states, impacting various aspects of global governance. This subchapter delves into the reshaping of global governance structures in the face of political fragmentation, addressing the concerns of diplomats and economists.

One of the key areas of focus is the economic implications of successful secessionist movements. This section analyzes the impact on trade, economy, and financial systems if all secessionist movements were to achieve independence. It explores the potential disruptions to established economic relationships, the challenges of establishing new trade agreements, and the effects on financial stability.

Political fragmentation also has significant implications for diplomatic relations, alliances, and regional power dynamics. This subchapter examines the potential consequences of multiple independent states emerging from secessionist movements. It delves into the complexities of redefining diplomatic relations, the formation of new alliances, and the potential shifts in regional power dynamics.

Cultural preservation is another crucial aspect to consider within newly independent states resulting from secessionist movements. This section focuses on the preservation and promotion of distinct cultures, addressing the challenges of maintaining cultural identity amidst political fragmentation.

The subchapter also explores the national security challenges posed by multiple independent states. It investigates potential border disputes, the formation of defense alliances, and the implications for regional stability. It provides a comprehensive analysis of the security implications and the measures that need to be taken to ensure stability in a fragmented political landscape.

Another critical area of examination is resource management. This section analyzes how resource-rich regions seeking independence could impact global resource distribution, energy security, and environmental policies. It highlights the potential challenges and opportunities in managing resources in a fragmented political environment.

The protection of minority rights within newly independent states is a pressing issue that needs to be addressed. This subchapter investigates the potential conflicts and challenges in ensuring inclusivity and safeguarding minority rights. It emphasizes the importance of addressing these concerns to maintain stability and harmony within the newly independent states.

Governance and institution-building are significant challenges that arise from successful secessionist movements. This section explores the opportunities and obstacles in establishing new governments, legal systems, and institutions. It examines the process of institution-building and the potential for creating resilient and effective governance structures.

The subchapter also assesses the processes and implications of international recognition of newly independent states. It explores their participation in global organizations and treaties, the challenges they face in gaining recognition, and the impact on global governance structures.

Socioeconomic disparities are likely to emerge between newly independent states and their counterparts. This section investigates the potential for widening disparities in wealth, development, and social services. It highlights the importance of addressing these disparities to ensure stability and sustainable development.

Overall, this subchapter provides a comprehensive analysis of the consequences of political fragmentation on global governance structures. It addresses the concerns of diplomats and economists, offering insights into the challenges and opportunities that arise from successful secessionist movements. By understanding these implications, policymakers can make informed decisions to navigate the complexities of a fragmented political landscape.

www.ingramcontent.com/pod-product-compliance
Lightning Source LLC
Chambersburg PA
CBHW051252160726
47994CB00003B/1133